Name it

An Author's Book for Characters

Copyright © 2019 by

TEECEE Design Studio©

All rights reserved. This book or any portion thereof may not be reproduced or used in any manner whatsoever without the express written permission of the publisher except for the use of brief quotations in a book review.

First Print, 2019

Character Name

Major Character

Also Known By

Minor Character

Age

Distinguishing Marks

Height

Weight

In Which Book Used

Eye Colour

Extra Notes

Hair Colour

Hair Style

Body Build

<table>
<tr><td>

Character Name

</td><td>

Major Character

</td></tr>
<tr><td>

Also Known By

</td><td>

Minor Character

</td></tr>
<tr><td>

Age

Height

</td><td>

Distinguishing Marks

</td></tr>
<tr><td>

Weight

</td><td>

In Which Book Used

</td></tr>
<tr><td>

Eye Colour

Hair Colour

Hair Style

Body Build

</td><td>

Extra Notes

</td></tr>
</table>

Character Name

Major Character

Also Known By

Minor Character

Age

Distinguishing Marks

Height

Weight

In Which Book Used

Eye Colour

Extra Notes

Hair Colour

Hair Style

Body Build

Character Name

Major Character

Also Known By

Minor Character

Age

Height

Distinguishing Marks

Weight

In Which Book Used

Eye Colour

Extra Notes

Hair Colour

Hair Style

Body Build

CHARACTER NAME	MAJOR CHARACTER
ALSO KNOWN BY	MINOR CHARACTER
AGE	DISTINGUISHING MARKS
HEIGHT	
WEIGHT	IN WHICH BOOK USED
EYE COLOUR	EXTRA NOTES
HAIR COLOUR	
HAIR STYLE	
BODY BUILD	

Character Name

Major Character

Also Known By

Minor Character

Age

Distinguishing Marks

Height

Weight

In Which Book Used

Eye Colour

Extra Notes

Hair Colour

Hair Style

Body Build

Character Name

Major Character

Also Known By

Minor Character

Age

Distinguishing Marks

Height

Weight

In Which Book Used

Eye Colour

Extra Notes

Hair Colour

Hair Style

Body Build

Character Name

Major Character

Also Known By

Minor Character

Age

Distinguishing Marks

Height

Weight

In Which Book Used

Eye Colour

Extra Notes

Hair Colour

Hair Style

Body Build

CHARACTER NAME

MAJOR CHARACTER

ALSO KNOWN BY

MINOR CHARACTER

AGE

DISTINGUISHING MARKS

HEIGHT

WEIGHT

IN WHICH BOOK USED

EYE COLOUR

EXTRA NOTES

HAIR COLOUR

HAIR STYLE

BODY BUILD

Character Name

Major Character

Also Known By

Minor Character

Age

Distinguishing Marks

Height

Weight

In Which Book Used

Eye Colour

Extra Notes

Hair Colour

Hair Style

Body Build

Character Name	Major Character

Also Known By	Minor Character

Age	Distinguishing Marks

Height	

Weight	In Which Book Used

Eye Colour	Extra Notes

Hair Colour	

Hair Style	

Body Build	

Character Name	Major Character

Also Known By	Minor Character

Age	Distinguishing Marks

Height	

Weight	In Which Book Used

Eye Colour	Extra Notes

Hair Colour

Hair Style

Body Build

Character Name

Major Character

Also Known By

Minor Character

Age

Distinguishing Marks

Height

Weight

In Which Book Used

Eye Colour

Extra Notes

Hair Colour

Hair Style

Body Build

Character Name	Major Character

Also Known By

Minor Character

Age

Distinguishing Marks

Height

Weight

In Which Book Used

Eye Colour

Extra Notes

Hair Colour

Hair Style

Body Build

Character Name

Major Character

Also Known By

Minor Character

Age

Distinguishing Marks

Height

Weight

In Which Book Used

Eye Colour

Extra Notes

Hair Colour

Hair Style

Body Build

Character Name

Major Character

Also Known By

Minor Character

Age

Distinguishing Marks

Height

Weight

In Which Book Used

Eye Colour

Extra Notes

Hair Colour

Hair Style

Body Build

Character Name

Major Character

Also Known By

Minor Character

Age

Distinguishing Marks

Height

Weight

In Which Book Used

Eye Colour

Extra Notes

Hair Colour

Hair Style

Body Build

Character Name

Major Character

Also Known By

Minor Character

Age

Distinguishing Marks

Height

Weight

In Which Book Used

Eye Colour

Extra Notes

Hair Colour

Hair Style

Body Build

Character Name	Major Character
Also Known By	Minor Character
Age	Distinguishing Marks
Height	
Weight	In Which Book Used
Eye Colour	Extra Notes
Hair Colour	
Hair Style	
Body Build	

Character Name

Major Character

Also Known By

Minor Character

Age

Distinguishing Marks

Height

Weight

In Which Book Used

Eye Colour

Extra Notes

Hair Colour

Hair Style

Body Build

| Character Name | Major Character |

| Also Known By | Minor Character |

| Age | Distinguishing Marks |

| Height | |

| Weight | In Which Book Used |

| Eye Colour | Extra Notes |

| Hair Colour | |

| Hair Style | |

| Body Build | |

Character Name

Major Character

Also Known By

Minor Character

Age

Distinguishing Marks

Height

Weight

In Which Book Used

Eye Colour

Extra Notes

Hair Colour

Hair Style

Body Build

<table>
<tr><td>

CHARACTER NAME

HEIGHT

WEIGHT

EYE COLOUR

HAIR COLOUR

HAIR STYLE

BODY BUILD

</td></tr>
</table>

CHARACTER NAME	MAJOR CHARACTER
ALSO KNOWN BY	MINOR CHARACTER
AGE	DISTINGUISHING MARKS
HEIGHT	
WEIGHT	IN WHICH BOOK USED
EYE COLOUR	EXTRA NOTES
HAIR COLOUR	
HAIR STYLE	
BODY BUILD	

Character Name

Also Known By

Age

Height

Weight

Eye Colour

Hair Colour

Hair Style

Body Build

Major Character

Minor Character

Distinguishing Marks

In Which Book Used

Extra Notes

Character Name	Major Character

Also Known By	Minor Character

Age

Distinguishing Marks

Height

Weight

In Which Book Used

Eye Colour

Extra Notes

Hair Colour

Hair Style

Body Build

Character Name

Major Character

Also Known By

Minor Character

Age

Distinguishing Marks

Height

Weight

In Which Book Used

Eye Colour

Extra Notes

Hair Colour

Hair Style

Body Build

<table>
<tr><td>

Character Name

Also Known By

Age

Height

Weight

Eye Colour

Hair Colour

Hair Style

Body Build

</td><td>

Major Character

Minor Character

Distinguishing Marks

In Which Book Used

Extra Notes

</td></tr>
</table>

Character Name

Major Character

Also Known By

Minor Character

Age

Distinguishing Marks

Height

Weight

In Which Book Used

Eye Colour

Extra Notes

Hair Colour

Hair Style

Body Build

Character Name

Major Character

Also Known By

Minor Character

Age

Distinguishing Marks

Height

Weight

In Which Book Used

Eye Colour

Extra Notes

Hair Colour

Hair Style

Body Build

Character Name

Major Character

Also Known By

Minor Character

Age

Distinguishing Marks

Height

Weight

In Which Book Used

Eye Colour

Extra Notes

Hair Colour

Hair Style

Body Build

Character Name

Major Character

Also Known By

Minor Character

Age

Distinguishing Marks

Height

Weight

In Which Book Used

Eye Colour

Extra Notes

Hair Colour

Hair Style

Body Build

Character Name

Major Character

Also Known By

Minor Character

Age

Distinguishing Marks

Height

Weight

In Which Book Used

Eye Colour

Extra Notes

Hair Colour

Hair Style

Body Build

Character Name

Major Character

Also Known By

Minor Character

Age

Distinguishing Marks

Height

Weight

In Which Book Used

Eye Colour

Extra Notes

Hair Colour

Hair Style

Body Build

Character Name

Major Character

Also Known By

Minor Character

Age

Height

Distinguishing Marks

Weight

In Which Book Used

Eye Colour

Extra Notes

Hair Colour

Hair Style

Body Build

Character Name

Major Character

Also Known By

Minor Character

Age

Distinguishing Marks

Height

Weight

In Which Book Used

Eye Colour

Extra Notes

Hair Colour

Hair Style

Body Build

Character Name

Major Character

Also Known By

Minor Character

Age

Distinguishing Marks

Height

Weight

In Which Book Used

Eye Colour

Extra Notes

Hair Colour

Hair Style

Body Build

Character Name

Major Character

Also Known By

Minor Character

Age

Distinguishing Marks

Height

Weight

In Which Book Used

Eye Colour

Extra Notes

Hair Colour

Hair Style

Body Build

Character Name	Major Character

Also Known By	Minor Character

Age

Height

Distinguishing Marks

Weight

In Which Book Used

Eye Colour

Extra Notes

Hair Colour

Hair Style

Body Build

Character Name

Major Character

Also Known By

Minor Character

Age

Distinguishing Marks

Height

Weight

In Which Book Used

Eye Colour

Extra Notes

Hair Colour

Hair Style

Body Build

Character Name	Major Character

Also Known By	Minor Character

Age	Distinguishing Marks

Height

Weight

In Which Book Used

Eye Colour

Extra Notes

Hair Colour

Hair Style

Body Build

Character Name

Major Character

Also Known By

Minor Character

Age

Distinguishing Marks

Height

Weight

In Which Book Used

Eye Colour

Extra Notes

Hair Colour

Hair Style

Body Build

| Character Name | Major Character |

| Also Known By | Minor Character |

| Age | Distinguishing Marks |

| Height | |

| Weight | In Which Book Used |

| Eye Colour | Extra Notes |

| Hair Colour | |

| Hair Style | |

| Body Build | |

<table>
<tr><td>

Character Name

</td><td>

Major Character

</td></tr>
<tr><td>

Also Known By

</td><td>

Minor Character

</td></tr>
</table>

Character Name

Major Character

Also Known By

Minor Character

Age

Distinguishing Marks

Height

Weight

In Which Book Used

Eye Colour

Extra Notes

Hair Colour

Hair Style

Body Build

Character Name

[ ]

Also Known By

[ ]

Age

[ ]

Height

[ ]

Weight

[ ]

Eye Colour

[ ]

Hair Colour

[ ]

Hair Style

[ ]

Body Build

[ ]

Major Character

[ ]

Minor Character

[ ]

Distinguishing Marks

[ ]

In Which Book Used

[ ]

Extra Notes

[ ]

| CHARACTER NAME | MAJOR CHARACTER |

| ALSO KNOWN BY | MINOR CHARACTER |

| AGE | DISTINGUISHING MARKS |

HEIGHT

| WEIGHT | IN WHICH BOOK USED |

| EYE COLOUR | EXTRA NOTES |

HAIR COLOUR

HAIR STYLE

BODY BUILD

Character Name	Major Character
Also Known By	Minor Character
Age	Distinguishing Marks
Height	
Weight	In Which Book Used
Eye Colour	Extra Notes
Hair Colour	
Hair Style	
Body Build	

Character Name

Major Character

Also Known By

Minor Character

Age

Distinguishing Marks

Height

Weight

In Which Book Used

Eye Colour

Extra Notes

Hair Colour

Hair Style

Body Build

Character Name

Major Character

Also Known By

Minor Character

Age

Distinguishing Marks

Height

Weight

In Which Book Used

Eye Colour

Extra Notes

Hair Colour

Hair Style

Body Build

CHARACTER NAME	MAJOR CHARACTER

ALSO KNOWN BY	MINOR CHARACTER

AGE

HEIGHT

DISTINGUISHING MARKS

WEIGHT

IN WHICH BOOK USED

EYE COLOUR

EXTRA NOTES

HAIR COLOUR

HAIR STYLE

BODY BUILD

Character Name

Major Character

Also Known By

Minor Character

Age

Distinguishing Marks

Height

Weight

In Which Book Used

Eye Colour

Extra Notes

Hair Colour

Hair Style

Body Build

CHARACTER NAME

MAJOR CHARACTER

ALSO KNOWN BY

MINOR CHARACTER

AGE

DISTINGUISHING MARKS

HEIGHT

WEIGHT

IN WHICH BOOK USED

EYE COLOUR

EXTRA NOTES

HAIR COLOUR

HAIR STYLE

BODY BUILD

Character Name	Major Character

Also Known By

Minor Character

Age

Distinguishing Marks

Height

Weight

In Which Book Used

Eye Colour

Extra Notes

Hair Colour

Hair Style

Body Build

Character Name

Major Character

Also Known By

Minor Character

Age

Distinguishing Marks

Height

Weight

In Which Book Used

Eye Colour

Extra Notes

Hair Colour

Hair Style

Body Build

Character Name	Major Character

Also Known By	Minor Character

Age	Distinguishing Marks

Height

Weight	In Which Book Used

Eye Colour	Extra Notes

Hair Colour

Hair Style

Body Build

Character Name

Major Character

Also Known By

Minor Character

Age

Distinguishing Marks

Height

Weight

In Which Book Used

Eye Colour

Extra Notes

Hair Colour

Hair Style

Body Build

Character Name

Major Character

Also Known By

Minor Character

Age

Distinguishing Marks

Height

Weight

In Which Book Used

Eye Colour

Extra Notes

Hair Colour

Hair Style

Body Build

Character Name	Major Character

Also Known By	Minor Character

Age	Distinguishing Marks

Height

Weight

In Which Book Used

Eye Colour

Extra Notes

Hair Colour

Hair Style

Body Build

CHARACTER NAME

MAJOR CHARACTER

ALSO KNOWN BY

MINOR CHARACTER

AGE

DISTINGUISHING MARKS

HEIGHT

WEIGHT

IN WHICH BOOK USED

EYE COLOUR

EXTRA NOTES

HAIR COLOUR

HAIR STYLE

BODY BUILD

Character Name

Also Known By

Age

Height

Weight

Eye Colour

Hair Colour

Hair Style

Body Build

Major Character

Minor Character

Distinguishing Marks

In Which Book Used

Extra Notes

Character Name

Also Known By

Age

Height

Weight

Eye Colour

Hair Colour

Hair Style

Body Build

Major Character

Minor Character

Distinguishing Marks

In Which Book Used

Extra Notes

Character Name

Major Character

Also Known By

Minor Character

Age

Distinguishing Marks

Height

Weight

In Which Book Used

Eye Colour

Extra Notes

Hair Colour

Hair Style

Body Build

Character Name

Major Character

Also Known By

Minor Character

Age

Distinguishing Marks

Height

Weight

In Which Book Used

Eye Colour

Extra Notes

Hair Colour

Hair Style

Body Build

Character Name

Major Character

Also Known By

Minor Character

Age

Distinguishing Marks

Height

Weight

In Which Book Used

Eye Colour

Extra Notes

Hair Colour

Hair Style

Body Build

Character Name	Major Character

Also Known By	Minor Character

Age	Distinguishing Marks

Height

Weight

In Which Book Used

Eye Colour

Extra Notes

Hair Colour

Hair Style

Body Build

Character Name

Major Character

Also Known By

Minor Character

Age

Distinguishing Marks

Height

Weight

In Which Book Used

Eye Colour

Extra Notes

Hair Colour

Hair Style

Body Build

Character Name	Major Character
Also Known By	Minor Character
Age	Distinguishing Marks
Height	
Weight	In Which Book Used
Eye Colour	Extra Notes
Hair Colour	
Hair Style	
Body Build	

Character Name

Also Known By

Age

Height

Weight

Eye Colour

Hair Colour

Hair Style

Body Build

Major Character

Minor Character

Distinguishing Marks

In Which Book Used

Extra Notes

Character Name	Major Character

Also Known By	Minor Character

Age	Distinguishing Marks

Height

Weight | In Which Book Used

Eye Colour | Extra Notes

Hair Colour

Hair Style

Body Build

Character Name

Major Character

Also Known By

Minor Character

Age

Height

Distinguishing Marks

Weight

In Which Book Used

Eye Colour

Extra Notes

Hair Colour

Hair Style

Body Build

Character Name

Major Character

Also Known By

Minor Character

Age

Distinguishing Marks

Height

Weight

In Which Book Used

Eye Colour

Extra Notes

Hair Colour

Hair Style

Body Build

Character Name

Also Known By

Age

Height

Weight

Eye Colour

Hair Colour

Hair Style

Body Build

Major Character

Minor Character

Distinguishing Marks

In Which Book Used

Extra Notes

Character Name

Major Character

Also Known By

Minor Character

Age

Distinguishing Marks

Height

Weight

In Which Book Used

Eye Colour

Extra Notes

Hair Colour

Hair Style

Body Build

Character Name

Major Character

Also Known By

Minor Character

Age

Distinguishing Marks

Height

Weight

In Which Book Used

Eye Colour

Extra Notes

Hair Colour

Hair Style

Body Build

Character Name	Major Character

Also Known By	Minor Character

Age	Distinguishing Marks

Height

Weight

In Which Book Used

Eye Colour

Extra Notes

Hair Colour

Hair Style

Body Build

Character Name	Major Character

Also Known By	Minor Character

Age	Distinguishing Marks

Height

Weight	In Which Book Used

Eye Colour	Extra Notes

Hair Colour

Hair Style

Body Build

Character Name

Major Character

Also Known By

Minor Character

Age

Distinguishing Marks

Height

Weight

In Which Book Used

Eye Colour

Extra Notes

Hair Colour

Hair Style

Body Build

Character Name

Major Character

Also Known By

Minor Character

Age

Distinguishing Marks

Height

Weight

In Which Book Used

Eye Colour

Extra Notes

Hair Colour

Hair Style

Body Build

Character Name

Major Character

Also Known By

Minor Character

Age

Distinguishing Marks

Height

Weight

In Which Book Used

Eye Colour

Extra Notes

Hair Colour

Hair Style

Body Build

CHARACTER NAME	MAJOR CHARACTER

ALSO KNOWN BY	MINOR CHARACTER

AGE

HEIGHT

DISTINGUISHING MARKS

WEIGHT

IN WHICH BOOK USED

EYE COLOUR

EXTRA NOTES

HAIR COLOUR

HAIR STYLE

BODY BUILD

Character Name

Major Character

Also Known By

Minor Character

Age

Distinguishing Marks

Height

Weight

In Which Book Used

Eye Colour

Extra Notes

Hair Colour

Hair Style

Body Build

Character Name

Major Character

Also Known By

Minor Character

Age

Distinguishing Marks

Height

Weight

In Which Book Used

Eye Colour

Extra Notes

Hair Colour

Hair Style

Body Build

Character Name

Major Character

Also Known By

Minor Character

Age

Distinguishing Marks

Height

Weight

In Which Book Used

Eye Colour

Extra Notes

Hair Colour

Hair Style

Body Build

Character Name

Also Known By

Age

Height

Weight

Eye Colour

Hair Colour

Hair Style

Body Build

Major Character

Minor Character

Distinguishing Marks

In Which Book Used

Extra Notes

Character Name

Also Known By

Age

Height

Weight

Eye Colour

Hair Colour

Hair Style

Body Build

Major Character

Minor Character

Distinguishing Marks

In Which Book Used

Extra Notes

Character Name	**Major Character**

Also Known By	**Minor Character**

Age	**Distinguishing Marks**

Height

Weight

In Which Book Used

Eye Colour

Extra Notes

Hair Colour

Hair Style

Body Build

Character Name	Major Character

Also Known By	Minor Character

Age	Distinguishing Marks

Height

Weight | **In Which Book Used**

Eye Colour | **Extra Notes**

Hair Colour

Hair Style

Body Build

Character Name

Also Known By

Age

Height

Weight

Eye Colour

Hair Colour

Hair Style

Body Build

Major Character

Minor Character

Distinguishing Marks

In Which Book Used

Extra Notes

Character Name	Major Character

Also Known By	Minor Character

Age	Distinguishing Marks

Height

Weight

In Which Book Used

Eye Colour

Extra Notes

Hair Colour

Hair Style

Body Build

Character Name

Major Character

Also Known By

Minor Character

Age

Distinguishing Marks

Height

Weight

In Which Book Used

Eye Colour

Extra Notes

Hair Colour

Hair Style

Body Build

Character Name	Major Character

Also Known By	Minor Character

Age	Distinguishing Marks

Height

Weight

In Which Book Used

Eye Colour

Extra Notes

Hair Colour

Hair Style

Body Build

CHARACTER NAME

MAJOR CHARACTER

ALSO KNOWN BY

MINOR CHARACTER

AGE

DISTINGUISHING MARKS

HEIGHT

WEIGHT

IN WHICH BOOK USED

EYE COLOUR

EXTRA NOTES

HAIR COLOUR

HAIR STYLE

BODY BUILD

Character Name

Major Character

Also Known By

Minor Character

Age

Distinguishing Marks

Height

Weight

In Which Book Used

Eye Colour

Extra Notes

Hair Colour

Hair Style

Body Build

Character Name

____

Also Known By

____

Age

____

Height

____

Weight

____

Eye Colour

____

Hair Colour

____

Hair Style

____

Body Build

____

Major Character

____

Minor Character

____

Distinguishing Marks

____

In Which Book Used

____

Extra Notes

____

Character Name	**Major Character**
Also Known By	**Minor Character**
Age	**Distinguishing Marks**
Height	
Weight	**In Which Book Used**
Eye Colour	**Extra Notes**
Hair Colour	
Hair Style	
Body Build	

Character Name	Major Character

Also Known By	Minor Character

Age	Distinguishing Marks

Height

Weight | **In Which Book Used**

Eye Colour | **Extra Notes**

Hair Colour

Hair Style

Body Build

Character Name

Also Known By

Age

Height

Weight

Eye Colour

Hair Colour

Hair Style

Body Build

Major Character

Minor Character

Distinguishing Marks

In Which Book Used

Extra Notes

Character Name

Major Character

Also Known By

Minor Character

Age

Distinguishing Marks

Height

Weight

In Which Book Used

Eye Colour

Extra Notes

Hair Colour

Hair Style

Body Build

Character Name	Major Character
Also Known By	Minor Character
Age	Distinguishing Marks
Height	
Weight	In Which Book Used
Eye Colour	Extra Notes
Hair Colour	
Hair Style	
Body Build	

| Character Name | Major Character |

| Also Known By | Minor Character |

| Age | Distinguishing Marks |

Height

| Weight | In Which Book Used |

| Eye Colour | Extra Notes |

Hair Colour

Hair Style

Body Build

Character Name

Major Character

Also Known By

Minor Character

Age

Distinguishing Marks

Height

Weight

In Which Book Used

Eye Colour

Extra Notes

Hair Colour

Hair Style

Body Build

Thank you so much for your purchase.

I really do hope that this book has helped you,
even in some small way.

Would you like to see different designs/styles?

I am always very happy to hear from customers,
so please feel free to email me on

teeceedesignstudio@yahoo.com

www.ingramcontent.com/pod-product-compliance
Lightning Source LLC
Chambersburg PA
CBHW081310250726
48662CB00008B/2486